The Journey to Easter – and beyond

GW00598851

Other books in this series:

The Journey to Easter – and beyond

Sermons and Studies

John and Cynthia Tudor

The Westminster Experiment and Research
in Evangelism Trust
2011

Oxford Publishing Consultancy
12 Brookside
Headington
Oxford OX3 7PJ

ISBN 978-0-9555098-4-1

Typeset by Deltatype Ltd, Birkenhead, Merseyside
Printed in Great Britain by Information Press Ltd,
Southfield Road, Eynsham, Oxford OX29 4JB

Contents

Foreword

Sermons and Studies *by* John Tudor

Post-Easter studies relating the Resurrection to everyday living *by* Cynthia Tudor

Foreword

The series was given during the Passion and Easter season. It seeks to present the Holy Week and Easter message in both a biblical and contemporary fashion.

There are three sermons, one for Palm Sunday, Easter Sunday and the second Easter Sunday. Holy Week studies are based on the theology and message of the hymns we sing at this time.

Four studies on 'Lo, Jesus meets us . . .' in the contemporary world are set in the post-resurrection narrative of the Bible.

It was John's and my hope that the material would prove useful to preachers, leaders, groups and individuals as they, too, share in the essential heart of Christianity – the passion, death, and resurrection of Jesus Christ.

Cynthia Tudor

Publisher's Note

This book, and the other two books in the series – *Sermons for all Seasons* and *Singing our Faith* – has been published to honour the Revd. Dr R. John Tudor's ministry by the Westminster Experiment and Research into Evangelism Trust, of which he was the Chair for twenty-seven years.

As a part of the ongoing work of the Trust, it is hoped that churches will be able to raise money for their outreach through the sale of this, and the other two books.

Dedicated to
Revd Dois and Barbara Kennedy

and

Goddard Methodist Church
Fort Smith
Arkansas

Who is this?
This is Jesus the prophet from Nazareth.

Matthew 21:11

The place is Jerusalem, the ancient walled city. The time is Passover when it is estimated something like one and half million to two million people throng the city to celebrate the Jewish freedom and flight from Egypt. The mood is one of expectancy and excitement, and a section of the crowd are gloriously happy. The reason is one man. One man who chooses to enact a scene from the prophets.

The noise of excitement becomes a roar, and the people inside the city walls ask 'Who is this?', and the reply thunders back 'This is Jesus, the prophet from Nazareth.'

Amongst the many popular musicals shown on stage and film, there is one with the fascinating title *Stop the world I want to get off*. The lead sings 'Just once in a lifetime I feel like a giant … for this is my moment.'

Jesus is at long last saying to the world 'This is my moment.' Quietly, He has set His face to 'go to Jerusalem.' The gospel record is saying 'He set His face like flint' – so determined to go to Jerusalem at this precise moment of history. He chooses His moment at Passover. Meticulously He plans the day. Arrangements are made with a horse trader to release a donkey when the disciples give the password, 'The Lord has need of him.' He mounts and rides over the brow of the hill of the Mount of Olives. The crowd sees the significance, 'Behold your king comes unto you riding upon a donkey.' Children dance, youths climb palm trees and throw down the branches for people to wave. The crowd shout their hosannas. 'Who is this?' 'This is Jesus the prophet from Nazareth.'

Let us take a jet plane to the Middle East, and alight at

Cairo. Here we can see the pyramids and the Sphinx, and in the Museum the remarkable furnishings of the grave of Tutankhamun. We can marvel at the ancient Egyptian religion – the longest religion to last so many centuries. Yet, all based on the myths of legend and the stars, and now dead. Board the jet and fly to Athens, and climb to the Acropolis and reflect on Greek mythology – all now dead. If you wish, travel to Turkey to see the remains of Ephesus and the worship of Diana – all myth and legend, and all dead. Conclude the trip in Jerusalem – here walked Jesus; here He rode upon a donkey; here He taught; was betrayed and taken and crucified. There is no myth or legend. Jesus was a human being – bone of our bone and flesh of our flesh. He was born of Mary; became a refugee; grew up as a skilled builder in wood; conducted a ministry of preaching and healing with twelve followers. For three years He travelled his country; and then, on this Passover day, comes in triumph to Jerusalem. This is His moment in real time, in this world.

But Jesus is more than human – He is divine. He came humbly to be baptised by that fiery evangelist, John the Baptist. When John saw Jesus approaching, he said 'I cannot do this. I am not worthy.' Jesus insisted, and He related later how He heard a voice saying, 'This is my beloved Son.' Later He took three of His men to a mountain top where He became light itself. He was transfigured before them, and they understood His divine nature.

We sing on Palm Sunday, 'All glory laud and honour to Thee redeemer King.' He is our redeemer. The purpose of His coming to this world was to redeem the human family, to restore the human family to fellowship with our father, God. The meaning of redemption is clear.

When we do something wrong we get into trouble. Let it be fraud in Enron, a crime, and at school or college bad academic work will be met with discipline. We have to pay the price for our wrongs. The whole of humanity has done wrong – the evidence is everywhere – fraud in commerce, drug abuse, child pornography, domestic violence, wrong relationships. Above all, a failure to recognise God to whom we are answerable for our lives. There is no way we can rid ourselves of the shame and guilt. No sacrifice of ours could measure up to the sin; no financial gift could buy our freedom from sin. So, Jesus takes it upon Himself to pay the price by willingly going to the cross.

> There was no other good enough to pay the price of sin,
> He only could unlock the gate of heaven and let us in.

So, we are redeemed. The soldiers driving in those cruel nails heard Him say, 'Father forgive them for they know not what they do.' The dying thief pleaded that his sins could be forgiven and forgotten when he asked from his cross, 'Lord remember me when you come into your kingdom.', and Jesus redeeming replied, 'Today you will be with me in paradise.'

So, the Son of Man and the Son of God comes on this day to complete the reason for His incarnation. On Palm Sunday He is saying to the world 'This is my moment.' 'For this purpose did I come.' For us all there comes a moment to believe. In *The Times*, Derek Draper wrote of his moment happening in the beauty and quiet of St Margaret's Church, Westminster. As a lobbyist and highflier he had enjoyed an enviable lifestyle, but he had found it ultimately to be unsatisfactory. He dropped into St Margaret's. He found himself after a while praying and discovering the presence of a loving God.

Just once in a lifetime there comes that transforming moment, and life is never the same again.

Who is this? This is Jesus, the prophet from Nazareth

Beneath the cross of Jesus I fain would take my stand.

Galatians 6:1-18

It is very easy to sing our hymns without realising their depth of meaning. There now follow studies on some of the Passiontide hymns, seeking to understand how they came to be written and what they offer in a contemporary setting.

Beneath the cross of Jesus

The Victorian era influenced every part of English life. The British Empire was growing – Queen Victoria was made Empress of India. The Industrial Revolution brought wealth to the few, and hard working conditions to the many. The non-conformist Churches enjoyed considerable growth, whilst the Church of England experienced the struggle between low and high churchmanship. Powerful politicians like Gladstone and Disraeli had their day.

In an odd sort of way Victorian hymns often encapsulate such an atmosphere. Elizabeth Clephane, the author of 'Beneath the cross of Jesus' was born in 1830 in Edinburgh, but grew up in Melrose – Sir Walter Scott territory. Suffering from ill health she gave herself, because of her Christian faith, to the care of the needy and destitute. It is said that she once sold her own pony and trap to provide for an impoverished family. Each verse of the hymn becomes very personal.

> Beneath the cross of Jesus I fain would take my stand,
> The shadow of a mighty rock within a weary land;
> A home within the wilderness, a rest upon the way,
> From the burning of the noontide heat, and the burden
> of the day.

She is not well, her aching body and tired limbs, her lack of energy come through almost every line and word. The sheer strain of living in 'a weary land, a home in a wilderness, bearing the burden of the day.' How can she cope? It is beneath the cross she gladly takes her stand, and draws from it strength for living. She uses biblical illustrations from Isaiah: 'Behold a king will reign in righteousness, there will be streams in the desert, shade from a mighty rock in a weary land.' For her, life in her Victorian world is life lived in the desert of human poverty and need. Does she find in her experience something parallel to that of Jesus ministering to the poor and broken of His day?

> Upon that cross of Jesus my eye at times can see
> The very dying form of One who suffered there for me;
> And from my stricken heart with tears, two wonders I
>   confess
> The wonders of redeeming love, and my own unworthiness.

This is a very personal impression of Jesus – the cross is now in the background of her thinking. In her mind's eye she sees the Christ suffering and dying for her; and she suddenly sees the wonder of God's redeeming love in the sacrifice for someone like herself who is just not worthy of such love. Christ is the *salvator mundi*, but He is also a personal saviour.

> I take O cross, thy shadow for my abiding place;
> I ask no other sunshine than the sunshine of His face;
> Content to let the world go by, to know no gain or loss,
> My sinful self my only shame, my glory all the cross.

This is the most dramatic moment in the whole work. Elizabeth Clephane addresses the cross, standing back and gazing at it with intensity of feeling. There are immediate contrasts: we are back to the shadow (of the mighty rock of the first verse) and then thrust into sunshine. This is the sunshine of the face of Christ.

We are left to wonder how we see the face of Jesus. What were His facial features? Paul says that when we look into the face of Jesus we see God Himself. His face brings the brightness of the sun into the darkened life she lives amongst the poor, hungry and those bruised in the slums of her town. So, let the world in its rush after the material, rush on. Or let the mood of just doing nothing be hers. She has only one ambition: to glory in the cross of Christ. It is the Christ who dies for her, and this is all that matters.

So, what do we glory in? This is a most pertinent question in our materialistic society. Holy Week brings us face to face with the most important issues of living.

When I survey the wondrous cross.

Philippians 3:3-16

This must be the best loved of all the Passiontide Hymns. Written by Isaac Watts it has won international praise and affection. Isaac Watts broke with all the old boring ways of hymnody, and put into his verses a very personal approach to the cross.

> When I survey the wondrous cross
> On which the Prince of Glory died,
> My richest gain I count but loss,
> And pour contempt on all my pride.

'When I survey' – in other words when I take a long hard look. We get a surveyor to view the garden for landscaping, and he takes his time. We are selling the house, and the buyers get their surveyor to take a long hard look at the property. We cannot be casual about our looking at the cross of Jesus, because it is a 'wondrous cross'. This seems a contradiction because the cross as an instrument of torture is one of the bloodiest ever to have been invented. It is not the beautiful piece of jewellery accompanying the glamorous evening wear of a fashion model. It is bloody.

The prince of glory line first read 'Where the young Prince of Glory died'. He was comparatively young, and He led a young people's movement looking and searching for a new world order, based on a deep and sincere love of God and of one's neighbour. Nothing that I possess is of worth compared to the cross. I have to bury my pride.

I see this as a word to those of us in the ministry, where pride can be so prevalent. I recall being asked to speak for a younger minister renowned for his skills as an impresario. Prior to going on stage, he addressed us, choir and everyone, with the words,

'Now let them see how good we are.' I know he was seeking to calm our nerves and do our best. But offering worship, leading people to the throne of God's Grace is not meant to 'Let them see how good we are.', but to see how wonderful is the love of God in Christ. The cross is the place to learn humility.

> Forbid it Lord that I should boast
> Save in the death of Christ my God,
> All the vain things that charm me most
> I sacrifice them to His blood.

The theme of our pride continues. How we love to talk of what we own, of the position we have arrived at at work, or in the club. We like to talk up our holidays, our new clothes. The only worthy boast for the Christian is to talk about the amazing love of the Christ, who dies for the sins of the world and is our personal Saviour. The preacher in Ecclesiastes writes 'Vanity of vanities; all is vanity.' How true this can be of our modern society; and it is worth giving time to consider the pathetic emptiness of what appears to be so important to us at certain times.

> See from His head, His hands, His feet,
> Sorrow and love flow mingled down.
> Did e'er such love and sorrow meet,
> Or thorns compose so rich a crown?

This is a very visual verse. We are asked to survey the cruel crown of thorns jammed onto His head, blood spurting from the wounds. Imagine the sheer agony and frustration of being unable to move it from His head. 'So rich a crown.' In the Tower of London there is the new magnificent display of the Crown Jewels. How they sparkle and dazzle the eye! But no crown compares to His crown.

Then we are asked to survey His hands. Those loving hands

which have blessed little children, touched the filthy leper, handled bread and poured wine, are now nailed to wood. He once worked with wood. Next to His feet, unable now to travel, for they, too, are nailed to wood. Isaiah wrote, 'How beautiful upon the mountains are the feet of Him that brings good tidings, that publishes peace.' In our sin we nailed His feet, confined His movements, until in His resurrection He was let loose again in the world.

> Were the whole realm of nature mine
> That were an offering far too small.
> Love so amazing, so divine,
> Demands my soul, my life, my all.

The verse says it all. Harry Secombe used to sing 'If I ruled the world'; and, if we did, even that would be an insufficient gift in return for all that Christ has done for us on the 'wondrous cross'. Notice how Watts insists on the word 'demand'. There is no suggestion that we might treat this matter as a possibility. Or that we might be indifferent to the suffering Christ. On the contrary this wondrous cross demands that we give our utmost loyalty to the prince of glory.

One day the Cardinal was preaching in Notre Dame Cathedral in Paris and he told how a group of youths, the worse for drink, came into the cathedral and one of them was dared to go and kneel before a statue of the crucifixion and say, 'All this you did for me, and I don't give a damn.' The young man knelt, burst into tears, and he became your preacher today.

'Demands my soul, my life, my all.' Not just for now, but for all eternity.

O love divine, what hast thou done?

1 Peter 2:21-25, Ephesians 1:3-14

Charles Wesley wrote many memorable hymns for the Passion season. This truly great hymn, unfortunately not well known by congregations, had several more verses in the original version.

Wesley is in that great tradition of English hymn writers who express the very depths of understanding of the crucifixion and the suffering of our Lord. From the early days of the Roman Catholic Church in England, verse and music and art had made their mark on the English psyche. When Henry VIII took it upon himself to separate from Rome, and the twin branches of Anglicanism (low and high to put matters in their simplest form) developed, the theology of the cross continued. That is why protestant writers were able to write so movingly. I recall how at Westminster Cardinal Basil Hume would share with me each Lent the hymns of Charles Wesley.

Four years after his conversion on 21st May 1738, Charles Wesley published his *Hymns and Sacred Songs*, and included three under the heading 'Desiring to love.' The opening line is a direct quote from St Ignatius, and the theology of the hymn is based upon John 19:34-35. Christ is on the cross, the soldier's spear pierces His side, and the blood and water flow from the wound.

> O Love Divine what hast Thou done?
> The Immortal God has died for me.
> The Father's co-eternal Son
> Bore all my sins upon the tree.
> The Immortal God for me has died
> My Lord, my Love, is crucified.

An incredible paradox. The immortal God has died! We are the mystery of which Paul writes in Philippians, where 'Christ did not wish to remain on an equal with God but emptied Himself and took upon Himself the form of a servant who was crucified and who has returned to be in Glory'. In the process, Jesus has carried all my sins upon the tree – a term found for the cross in both Peter and Paul. The skill of Charles Wesley is that he brings a moment in history to this present time – he does not write 'Jesus my Lord *was* crucified', but 'Jesus my Lord *is* crucified'. So the cross is relevant *now* in my time, my generation. Of course there will be a cross in heaven until we humans are cleansed from all our sins, and we no longer continue to break the divine heart.

> Is crucified for me and you
> To bring us rebels back to God.
> Believe, believe the record true
> You all are bought in Jesu's blood,
> Pardon for all flows from His side
> My Lord, my Love is crucified.

Note the salient points: the rebels are humanity, the record is the scripture evidence. All are bought: the emphasis is on *all,* echoing the Arminian doctrine of grace being available to everyone, rather than the predestinarian view (current at the time of the controversy with George Whitfield) to only the elect. The blood is that of the New Covenant in Jeremiah 31:31, and referred to by Jesus at His last supper. The blood and the water flow from His side. Blood sacrificed for our sins, water to wash away sin in baptism.

> Behold Him all ye that pass by
> The bleeding Prince of life and peace.
> Come sinners see your Saviour die
> And say 'Was ever grief like His?'
> Come feel with me His blood applied
> My Lord, my Love is crucified.

Behold! Here is something to look at, to ponder, and all in the present tense! The bleeding prince of life has a peculiar relevance to our current climate of blood letting through terrorism and the frightening weapons of modern warfare. We are used to the bleeding of the human race. But the prince bleeds for love of the human race to save it from its bloodshed and inhumanity. And further, to bring us all to that blessedness of eternal life with God, free from sin and the fear of death. He is the prince of life indeed: 'I am the way, the truth and the life', 'I am come that you might have abundant living.'

Nothing compares to His grief – rejected and bruised and broken. Sense now for yourself, writes Wesley with real poignancy, that Christ's blood is shed. 'My Love' – the one who owns my heart and my life – He is crucified. Come and feel for yourself.

In other editions of this hymn, there is a further verse which movingly sums up the mood of this deeply moving work of the newly converted Charles Wesley:

> Then let us stand beneath the cross
> And feel His love and healing stream,
> All things for Him account but loss,
> And give up all our hearts to Him.
> Of nothing think or speak beside,
> My Lord, my Love is crucified.

O sacred head sore wounded.

Isaiah 53:5

There is no doubt that this is one of the most powerful and moving of the Passiontide hymns. There are at least three reasons for this. To begin with we have magnificent poetry, and this despite the translation from Latin to German to English. Then, secondly, each verse is packed with biblical and theological ideas. Thirdly, we sing the hymn to the wonderfully strong Bach chorale.

The origins are somewhat vague because this is a lengthy poem emerging from the mists of medieval times. Credit is given to St Bernard of Clairvaux, the extraordinary and highly gifted monk whose dates are 1090–1153. Born of an aristocratic family, he entered a Cistercian monastery when he was twenty-two. His followers grew in number so quickly that three years later he headed a new monastery in the Vale of Clairvaux. His fame meant he was consulted by the pope, kings and church leaders. He was prominent in the crusades. His devotional hymns are very beautiful. Martin Luther said of St Bernard, 'He was the best monk who ever lived – whom I love beyond all the rest.'

The original work consisted of seven sections, although modern hymn books contain much reduced versions. First translated into German from the Latin by Paul Gerhardt (1656) it was then put into English by the Princeton professor J.W. Alexander, who was born in Virginia in 1804.

The seven sections were addressed to the crucified Christ – His feet, knees, hands, side, heart, breast, and head, where our version begins.

O sacred head sore wounded, with grief and shame weighed down,
Now scornfully surrounded with thorns, Thine only crown.
How pale Thou art with anguish, with sore abuse and scorn,

How does that visage languish, which once was bright as
morn.

Our minds immediately go to the medieval portrayals of the
suffering Christ in painting and sculpture. The stark reality of
suffering on the bloody cross, picked out with telling detail. The
biblical themes are all there from the suffering servant of Isaiah
– grief and shame: 'He was despised and rejected.' Scornfully
surrounded – the chief priests at Calvary screaming, 'He saved
others he cannot save himself.' The cruel crown of thorns and
the mocking of the soldiers. The visage which once was bright
as morn – the 'bright morning star' of the Book of Revelation.

 We are directly brought into the gloom and doom laden
atmosphere of the cross. Already there is a sense of dread and
the pervading question: 'Why?'

What Thou, my Lord, hast suffered was all for sinner's gain,
Mine, mine was the transgression, but Thine the deadly pain.
Lo, here I fall, my Saviour! 'Tis I deserve Thy place
Look on me with Thy favour, vouchsafe to me Thy grace.

Theologians write about the Work of Christ, namely the
redemption of the world, the fact that sin had to be faced and
overcome, and the inevitability of the willing sacrifice of Jesus.
The author now makes the cross a personal matter. Jesus is
'my Lord' and His suffering was for 'my gain'; 'I sinned', but
'Christ suffered.' Now before the cross 'I fall, for you are my
Saviour.' Then the two requests: 'Look on me with your favour'
reminds us of Jesus looking at John from the cross and asking
the disciple to take care of His mother, and also granting mercy
to the dying thief on the next cross, 'Today you will be with me
in paradise.' That gift of divine grace, love in action.

What language shall I borrow to thank Thee, dearest Friend
For this Thy drying sorrow, Thy pity without end?

O make me Thine forever, and should I fainting be,
Lord, let me never, never outlive my love *for* Thee.

There are occasions in life when words are not enough. In that
deep emotional moment when you want to say to your dearest,
'I love you', you still feel the words are not saying everything
you want to say. So, when we look at the Christ on the cross
seeking to understand His suffering and His love for us, what
words can ever by sufficient? Perhaps we do not thank Christ
as we should for His grace and self-sacrifice. It is so easy to take
all this for granted.

Then Jesus is our Friend! Jesus in the upper room, on the
night in which He was betrayed, said to His disciples, 'You
are my friends.' What an extraordinary thought. He who is the
Logos, the mind behind the universe, the son of the most high
God, can be my friend. He has shown how much He values that
friendship: 'No greater love can a man show than that he lays
down his life for his friends.' We love to sing 'What a Friend
we have in Jesus.' John Newton, after his amazing experiences
of the love of Christ, could write.

> Jesus! My Shepherd, Brother, Friend,
> My prophet, Priest and King,
> My Lord, my Life, my Way, my End,
> Accept the praise I bring.

Then comes the contrast between 'dying sorrow' and 'pity
without end'. The sorrow will die away, but never that divine
pity for the human race, and for the individual believer. So, as
Christ has loved, may our love be eternal too.

In the cross of Christ I glory.

Galatians 6:1-14

The Saturday after Good Friday is a strange day. We feel as though we are in limbo. Our feelings are different from those of the early disciples and the women of the gospel story. For them Jesus was dead. For us we already know the Easter story. Today Jesus lies in that borrowed tomb – tomorrow we will be singing praises. We shall be glorying in the prince of life. Long ago the disciples were going to be utterly bewildered, nervous and exhausted on that first day of the first week of the first Easter.

So now we can sing, 'In the cross of Christ I glory', written by a very extraordinary and gifted character. John Bowring was born in Exeter and his father owned a successful woollen company. Leaving school at fourteen, John entered the business and became very interested in foreign trade. By the age of sixteen he was conversant in five languages. When he died at the age of eighty he could speak 100 languages and was conversant with 200. He was a brilliant cultured scholar and became a Member of Parliament. Entering the Diplomatic Service he was Governor of Hong Kong, and British Envoy to Hawaii. In 1854 he was knighted. Throughout his extremely busy life he remained a thoroughly committed Christian, and was aware of the significance of the passion, death and resurrection of Jesus.

> In the cross of Christ I glory,
> Towering o'er the wrecks of time.
> All the light of sacred story
> Gathers round its head sublime.

So, it is not any cross. There were plenty of them wherever the Roman Empire went. When Jesus was a youngster, 12,000 of his countrymen were crucified after a revolt against the occupying power. No, it is not any cross! There is but one cross for

Bowring and all the followers of Jesus. The cross of Calvary. The theme reflects all the Passiontide hymns in refusing to see anything but glory in the cross despite the fact it was a wretched gibbet.

Empires come and go! Roman, Greek, Holy Roman, Spanish, German, British, and more, belong to history. The writing is on the wall already for the so-called great powers of today. New empires wait in the wings, but they will come and go. The constant factor, the dependable truth is that the cross of Christ will tower above them. This is a sacred and sublime story for all time.

> When the woes of life o'ertake me
> Friends deceive and fears annoy,
> Never shall the cross forsake me,
> Lo it glows with peace and joy.

Bowring's career saw him as a successful businessman, politician, diplomat, and scholar. He must have experienced endless pressures. He would be let down by so-called friends. At times he, no doubt, went in fear of his life during his travels. Yet his inspiration has been the cross and the Christ of Calvary. The 'light of sacred story' in the first verse produces a glow 'with peace and joy'.

Jesus has given His disciples precious gifts. The peace of Christ – 'peace I give to you, my peace I leave with you. Not as the world gives, give I to you.' 'Let not your heart be troubled. You believe in God, believe also in Me.' His is the 'peace which passes all understanding'. The joy of Christ, Jesus longed in that upper room for His followers to have His joy, that their joy may be full.

Peace and joy in adversity – these enduring gifts are available to any who would believe.

> When the sun of bliss is beaming
> Light and love upon my way,
> From the cross, the radiance streaming
> Adds more lustre to the day.

This verse is in total contrast to the last. Life has great and good moments, and one must not forget at such times how much Christ has done for us through His death and resurrection. In difficult times we turn to God. When life gets easier and brighter we tend to move away from God. When a nation is threatened, people attend church. When the dangers fade away, so do the people in their devotions. Bowring urges us not to forget the cross – its meaning will add a certain lustre to our day.

> Bane and blessing, pain and pleasure
> By the cross are sanctified;
> Peace is there that knows no measure,
> Joys that through all time abide.

Here is an interesting use of language, as Bowring takes two contrasting elements of our human experience, and uses the same letter for each couple. Bane and blessing, pain and pleasure. Bane is an old English word which means disaster. Whatever we have lived through, or are living through now, this verse brings together the experiences of the previous two.

Thus we are prepared for Easter day and all our days, until that moment we are called into the felicity of that higher service we describe as heaven.

He is risen.

Mark 16:6

Two questions come to mind about the first Easter Day. The first is what were the disciples doing? The second is, what were the women doing? Presumably the men were regrouping. We know about the women.

Forbidden by Jewish law to go near a corpse on the Sabbath, they could still be busy preparing sacrifices, flowers and sweet scented aromas for the tomb where their late Master lay. In the heat His body would decompose quickly and they wanted their preparations to smell so good.

So, while the dawn was streaking across the sky on that first day of the week, they slipped down the narrow Jerusalem streets and out to the tomb. Imagine their utter surprise to see the huge round stone rolled back. Imagine their fear when they saw God's messenger, and then their mixture of emotions when he said 'He is risen.'

For two thousand years, in good times and in bad, the Christian Church has proclaimed 'He is risen.' This is the very heart of the Christian faith.

In our study of hymns we looked at a somewhat unknown hymn of Charles Wesley, namely 'O Love divine, what hast Thou done?' Today, in common with Christians throughout Christendom, we sing the most popular of his Easter hymns 'Christ the Lord is risen today, Alleluia!' Let us look at the claims Wesley makes.

Love's redeeming work is done
Two things strike us immediately. The contrast between Good Friday and Easter Day. Good Friday was dark and foreboding. Jesus was tortured, scourged, rejected. He hung out to die with every lack of human dignity possible. No wonder 'darkness

covered the face of the earth'. And yet, in the gloom we saw the beauty of Christ's love: He prayed for the forgiveness of His executioners, He gave eternal hope to the dying thief 'today you will be with me in Paradise.' Now Easter Day dawns and all is light in His glorious resurrection.

The resurrection speaks to us supremely of Christ's eternal love, revealing once and for all that love is the greatest power. 'Love's redeeming work is done.' Evil did its damnedest in killing Jesus, the very Son of God. It believed it had put Him away for good. Death saw to that. But here is the risen Christ, and two obvious things have happened. Evil has been defeated and so, too, death.

But I can hear someone say, 'Come off it, Preacher. Anyone with any sense knows that evil is rampant in our contemporary society. How dare you claim evil has been defeated?' That is a very fair question. The Christian claim is that the resurrection of Jesus means that at the very heart of evil there is defeat. Let me use this illustration. Imagine the whole world of humanity lives in one huge forest or jungle. In the centre there is a clearing, and in the clearing an empty cross and an empty tomb. Christ is risen, and evil understands it cannot harm Him. He is eternal, He is the victory! Evil now reels back into the forest, and everywhere in the forest there are strong pockets of evil. Now Jesus Christ becomes dependent upon His followers. Each believer knows that evil in his or her heart has been overcome through Christ's abiding, saving presence. Our task is to tackle the evil with His divine help. One day it is our earnest desire and prayer that, 'One day the kingdoms of this world will become the kingdom of our God.'

We need to grasp the cataclysmic significance of the events of Easter: 'LOVE's redeeming work is done.'

Secondly, Charles Wesley invites us to 'soar where Christ has led.' This, then, will give us three wonderful gifts through the resurrection of our Lord. The gifts come in language which needs some explanation!

The first gift: ours the cross

We don't want a cross, but life will hand us one of one sort or another! We have a Christ who has suffered on the cross. Shared our pain, our rejection, our broken relationships. He has identified Himself with our suffering humanity, and this means our God understands our problems, our reactions.

In ministry I have had several husbands or wives coming to tell me their marriage vows have been betrayed, and the partner has left. One lady went through hell in her experience, but she maintained through it all that she had found strength to face life through the suffering Christ. 'God is so good,' was her constant theme.

We all face physical suffering. Some folk in every congregation will have had the good fortune not to suffer pain and distress. But the fact is one day they will! I know personally what it is to go through surgery, and the stress and strain, in the company of the risen Christ. Did He not say 'I am with you always.'

The second gift is the grave

Christ is risen, the grave is no longer to be feared. Our generation tries to push death away. We want the thrill of living. We have our cosmetic ranges to put off the ageing process. But we cannot. The end of breathing in our bodies is an experience we each have to face; and because of Easter, death is but a gateway through which we pass. When my dear friend Dame Thora Hird was near to her death, she said to me 'I am alright, He is with me.' Jesus in the upper room explained that He was going to 'prepare a place for us. Where I am, there you may be also.'

And the third gift: ours the skies

With the risen Christ ever present, life can be lived to the full. 'I am come that you might have life, and have it more abundantly.' The sky's the limit for the Christian. A life free of sin, free to serve one's fellows, free to relish the beauty and wonder of creation, free to love God and neighbour. Abundant living.

So in conclusion, because Christ is risen, Wesley writes we are 'To sing and to love'. What better ways of praising Christ and His victories over sin and death than by singing? Lifting up our voices in praise with Christians throughout the world.

But the praise doesn't end there. For Easter flowers and lilies in the sanctuary remind us of the company of Christ who is no longer with us in the flesh but in the spirit. That great company 'which no man can number' which, gathered round the throne of the lamb sing, 'Worthy is the lamb that was slain to receive honour and riches and wisdom and power.' The Church militant on earth joins with the Church triumphant in an unending hymn of praise because Divine Love is victorious.

> 'Till, added to that heavenly choir,
> We'll raise our songs of triumph higher,
> And praise Thee in a nobler strain,
> Out-soar the first-born seraph's flight,
> And sing with all our friends in light,
> Thine everlasting love to man'

Christ the Lord is risen today. Alleluia!

Unless – the magnificence of doubt.

John 20:25

We began our Easter sermon wondering what the disciples were doing when the women were preparing to take their spices to the tomb. Clearly they were regrouping and, as the day wore on, two of them left for Emmaus; and Thomas was missing.

Jesus came and stood among them, and the disciples 'were overjoyed when they saw the Lord.' Later Thomas arrived, and they told him what had happened. Immediately, he refused to believe them, 'Unless I can put my finger where the nails were in the marks of His hands, and put my hand into His side, I will not believe.'

A week goes by and this time Thomas is with the disciples, and Jesus comes and immediately addresses Thomas, 'Thomas, put your finger here; see my hands. Reach out your hand and put it in my side. Stop doubting and believe.' Thomas said to Him, 'My Lord and my God.' Jesus replied, 'Because you have seen, you have believed. Blessed are those who have not seen and yet believe.'

Doubt of the resurrection has been within the story of the Christian Church from its inception. Paul came to Athens and hired a lecture hall. So successful were his meetings that he was invited to address the great and the good of Athens in the Areopagus on Mars Hill, next to the Acropolis. He accepted and, using poetry and philosophy, he talked to them about God. He said, 'I passed by one of your altars. The inscription was "To the Unknown God".' 'I can let you know', went on Paul, 'of God who has made Himself known in the person of a man whom He has raised from the dead.' The members of the Areopagus roared with scornful laughter and refused to believe.

Paul established the Church in Corinth, and when he had

left he received news that the very foundation of the Church there, namely the death and resurrection of Jesus, was being questioned and even rejected. Hence his very stern, stiff letters to Corinth. He gives evidence for the resurrection by citing the witnesses by name, and finally by number and his own experience of the risen Christ. 'If Christ be not raised, then your faith is futile, you are still in your sin, death has its hold. BUT now is Christ raised from the dead.'

Go beyond the pages of scripture, and again and again in the story of Christianity there have been those like Thomas doubting the resurrection. Not least today in the current scientific atmosphere in which we live, and in the cynicism towards things of spiritual worth. Thomas – as the doubting Thomas is very much alive. We have to admire the gospel record. It is so honest. If the resurrection had been a concoction then all the followers would have believed with a great noise and fuss. But here, at the very outset of the resurrection movement, is Thomas – doubting – a disciple close to the heart of Jesus. Thank God for Thomas.

Our doubting belongs to the learning curve of life

From our youngest days we learn, to our cost, when we doubt the word of those who know better. Let me use a personal illustration. I was brought up in a manse family and was taught that if I did wrong I would be found out. I doubted this. We went to church three times on a Sunday when I was a child. In the afternoon I walked on my own to Junior Sunday School. On the way there was a machine selling chewing gum. For one halfpenny it dispensed one packet. For one penny it dispensed three. I set out on a grand scheme for improving my pocket money. I popped my penny collection into the machine, got three packets and sold them for the handsome profit of one halfpenny to my pals attending Sunday School. After several weeks my profits were increasing at a remarkable rate. But the Sunday School offertory was decreasing in the same proportion. I was found out. I didn't doubt any more that day that 'my sins would find me out.' The minister's son was expelled from Sunday School!

In my teens I turned my doubts to the scriptures and must have been a thorn in my father's side. I questioned his sermons. Especially around Easter. 'Prove it,' I used to say to him. Gently and firmly he tried to assuage my doubts; but when the day came to join the RAF for National Service I was ready 'to take wing'. No longer would I be bound up in all this church stuff and talk of resurrection. I was to live in the real world.

Drafted to training camp, the padre found me out. Insisted, despite my objections, that on Sundays I would be the choir (because all the previous draft had now left), and I would attend his Bible study every Monday. On the last Saturday Padre Hollis came to the billet and said to me, 'The local Minister is ill, and I have detailed you to take his Service tomorrow evening at such and such a church.' He thrust a paper in my hand: 'These are your hymns and Bible readings, and I've written out a sermon for you to read. The jeep will collect you and bring you back.' I got through the service, and the last hymn was, 'Take my life and let it be consecrated Lord to Thee.' As we sang it I thought, 'what a load of nonsense.' That night I never slept; and the following Monday morning I knelt in the camp chapel: His risen presence was very real. My doubts were gone. I had to offer for the ministry.

So, the Thomas story is of real significance to me. I hear the voice of the Christ saying, 'Blessed are those who have not seen but who believe.' I have not seen the risen Christ, but I know of His presence. It is so real.

But enough of Thomas for a moment. What Jesus did, and how He did it, in that room, tells me so much about the nature of Jesus, and therefore, of God His father. When He came to Thomas he wasn't critical. He didn't say, 'Well, you missed your chance.' He didn't condemn. He loved and dealt with Thomas in the way that Thomas could respond to. His love is truly wonderful.

It passes praises, that dear love of Thine!
My Saviour! Jesus! Yet this heart of mine
Would sing that love so full, so rich so free
Which brings a rebel sinner such as me, nigh unto God.

So, we take the leap of faith. Faith based on experience. We may not see Him, but we know of His presence. This doesn't mean we won't stop asking questions and arguing with God. A young man dies of a viral infection. We scream 'Oh God, why?' Then we discover that modern medicine (acting like God so often!) has no antidote to the virus! A family are killed in a car wreck at the weekend. 'O God, why?' Then we discover that the driver of the other car was a stupid character driving whilst drunk and stoned out of his mind.

There must have been times when Paul, having committed his life to Christ, had his moments of wondering and doubting. In that remarkable Chapter 8 of his Letter to the Romans he looks at all the things that could cause us to doubt. He uses a very interesting word. He writes 'But I am persuaded.' That is, he has reached this conclusion after many trials and tribulations: 'I am persuaded that there is nothing that can separate us from the love of God in Christ Jesus.'

So, we take the leap of faith like Thomas and we are spurred to action. There is a very strong tradition that Thomas travelled to south-west India and established Christianity. Hence the Mar Thoma Church.

So ours is a living faith in the presence of the Christ. We continue to be grateful to Jesus for those strength-giving words, 'Blessed are you Thomas, for you have seen and believed. Blessed are those who have not seen, and yet believed.'

No more we doubt Thee glorious Prince of life;
Life is nought without Thee; aid us in our strife,
Make us more than conquerors, through the deathless love;
Bring us safe through Jordan to Thy home above.

Lo, Jesus meets us risen from the tomb

Public was Death; but Power, but Might,
But Life again, but Victory,
Were hushed within the dead of night,
The shutter'd dark, the secrecy,
And all alone, alone, alone,
He rose again behind the stone.

Alice Meynell

On Easter Day we are full of Easter praise and hallelujahs, and rightly so. But what was it really like on that first Easter Morning? David Runcorn suggests that if we had been in Jerusalem at that time we would have slept right through it. 'We would have woken on the day of resurrection to just another morning "a day like any other".' I don't think that even the women and the disciples who discovered the empty tomb shouted 'hallelujah' at that moment. Their response was more muted and hesitant. Only as the day proceeded, and in the weeks that followed, was the full import of the empty tomb realised, as quietly Jesus met individuals and groups and they came to recognise Him as their risen Lord. (1 Corinthians 15:3-8)

In this series we eavesdrop on some of these meetings, and find 'Lo, Jesus meets us', too. Firstly, *in the upper room of fellowship*. (John 20:19-21)

The disciples were gathered behind locked doors. Imagine ten frightened, bewildered men. They had heard the rumours that the women had seen Jesus. But you can guess how they reacted to that! Some had been brave enough to go and see the empty tomb for themselves. Each one, no doubt, was recalling the trauma of the Thursday night and the Friday morning, and harbouring thoughts of the part they had played in the desertion, denial and betrayal of Jesus. In their hearts, perhaps, they were wondering if they were any different from that lost soul Judas. If Jesus was risen, did they really want to see Him? What would He say to them? They were a broken group, fragmented by the events of the past days, and not in the mood for shouting hallelujah! Then suddenly, Jesus was there saying 'Shalom, peace be with you.' There were no recriminations. He didn't blame anyone. He simply showed them the signs of His suffering; and the healing calm, and the love and forgiveness of His very presence begin to seep into their souls. Joy displaces fear. Not a happy-clappy exuberance, but the joyous wonder of a restored relationship that was beyond their wildest dreams, given all that they had said and done. They were united by their risen Lord.

We sing, 'Jesus stand among us in Thy risen power, Let this time of worship be a hallowed hour.' Jesus does meet us, wherever we gather in fellowship or worship. When we think about it, any group which comes together for worship, particularly if it is a larger more mixed bunch than the disciples: we may not have suffered the traumas the disciples had endured, but we come with various personal, emotional and spiritual needs. It may be for comfort or forgiveness, for hope or for assurance, or even challenge. We come at different stages on our spiritual pilgrimage: some just at the beginning of their Christian journey, others more mature in the faith. 'Lo, Jesus meets' each one of us in whatever condition we find ourselves when we meet in fellowship.

How? Perhaps this is a question we do not need to ask if we have shared together in meaningful worship. Lo, Jesus has met us in the music; in the spoken word; in the silence; in the touch or the look of other people. It was common in churches some time ago to see a sign in the pulpit bearing the words from St

John's Gospel 'Sir, we would see Jesus', as a reminder to the preacher of the purpose of worship. Those privileged to lead worship can be very humbled to discover that those gathered have indeed been touched in some way, i.e. 'they have seen Jesus'. As a leader they may have felt that they had not given of their best, but their inadequate and halting words have spoken to someone's need, and been a veritable benediction. However, all who are gathered together in fellowship can be the means, through what they say or are, by which someone may see Jesus. At the core and centre of fellowship is our own personal relationship with Jesus, and it is that which enables our fellowship to become richer, to embrace our differences and unite us in love.

There is a simple hymn which begins 'Turn your eyes upon Jesus'. When Jesus appeared to the first disciples in the upper room all eyes turned upon Him as He greeted them. When we meet in fellowship and turn towards Him, He can show us His hands and His side – the wounds that can heal us. We can hear His words 'Peace be with you', and know the joy of the presence of the risen Lord. Then we can sing with confidence, 'Lo, Jesus meets us risen from tomb, lovingly He greets us, scatters fear and gloom.' Hallelujah!

Lo, Jesus meets us in the garden of grief.

John 20:10-18

> It was unfinished.
> We stayed there, fixed, until the end,
> Women waiting for the body that we loved;
> and then it was unfinished.
> There was no time to cherish, cleanse, anoint;
> no time to handle him with love,
> no farewell.

Janet Morley

In our previous study we considered how Jesus meets us when we are gathered together in the fellowship of corporate worship. This study looks at the entirely different situation of an individual alone with her grief.

Part of the process of grieving after the passing of a loved one is the rite of the funeral itself. We frequently hear relatives of family members, who have disappeared and are presumed to have died, say that if only they could find the body and lay their loved one to rest, they could begin the process of recovery. Mary wanted to lay the body of Jesus to rest, to perform a last service for his broken body, and then learn to live with His loss. Therefore, she was totally distraught and literally blinded with grief when she came to look for the body, and embrace His death with love, to find that the tomb was empty, and there was only a gardener on the pathway. But it was there that Jesus met her and enabled her to recognise Him by the word 'Mary'. It was still not easy for her. He was raised beyond death to a different level of being; and she had to learn not to cling to the Jesus she had known in the past. But she knew without doubt that He was raised, and she had a gospel to proclaim.

In John Bowker's book *A year to live*, the title of one chapter is 'Easter comes at garden time'. A garden is a familiar image as a meeting place with God. For example, 'one is nearer God's heart in a garden', or 'I walked in the garden alone.' In John's Gospel we read, 'Now at the place where He was crucified, there was a garden, and in the garden, a new tomb.' If you have visited Jerusalem you have probably visited The Garden Tomb (that secluded area near the bus station). It is a garden created around rock tombs where there is also a large overhanging rock that has the appearance of a skull. Archaeological evidence suggests that Christ's tomb is really on the site of the Holy Sepulchre Church which echoes with the clangour of many tongues and varieties of music. Many pilgrims prefer the Garden Tomb where they can more easily commune with their risen Lord.

The new growth of spring flowers and foliage does bring hope after the darkness of winter, and can ease grief. Easter can come at garden time. In the novel *Springtime of the year* by Susan Hill, Ruth is struggling to cope with overwhelming grief after the death of her young husband in a tragic accident. She is shut up in herself with a total inability to accept any offers of help. At Easter her young brother-in-law urges her to carry out the tradition in her village of decorating the graves of loved ones with flowers on Holy Saturday. As she knelt beside her husband's grave, 'she thought then of that other body carried away from the terrible cross at dusk and the great stone rolled in front of the tomb, imagined how it must have been inside echoing and fusty as a cave, with the limp figure drained of all its blood and bound about in cloths. She felt within herself the bewilderment and fear and despair of those men and women.' After she had finished she stood back and said, 'tomorrow the sun will shine and the grave flowers will be like the raiment of the risen dead. But if He is risen, where do I find Him to see Him? How can I know?' The next day, Easter Day, she went to church 'and what she became aware of there, was not the presence of the village people sitting or kneeling behind her, but of others. The church was full of all those who had ever prayed in it, the air was crammed and vibrating with their goodness and the freedom and power of their resurrection.' For Ruth, her recovery had begun.

We do not have to be literally in a garden to experience grief or to meet Jesus in the midst of that grief. Grief can manifest itself anywhere. We can be blinded by it in a supermarket, at home, in our car, at work, wherever. The unbidden tears can flow and we can be swamped with self-pity. Such places can become a 'garden' if we can be aware of the presence of the risen Lord, and healing can begin. Charles Allen writes 'it is wonderful what God can do with a broken heart if we give Him all the pieces.' This is a simplification, perhaps, of a complex emotion and the awfulness of grief. But the core moment of our recovery must be when we realise that He is not the gardener, but our risen Lord.

> When our hearts are wintry, grieving or in pain,
> Thy touch may call us back to life again.
> Fields of our hearts that dead and bare have been.
>
> *J. M. C. Crum*

Lo, Jesus meets us on the road of reason.

Luke 24:13-32

Not to man, but God submit,
Lay my reasonings at Thy feet.

Charles Wesley

There was a real debate going on during that journey to Emmaus. Cleopas and his friend did not know what to make of all the stories and rumours that had been circulating in Jerusalem on that day. They had seen what Jesus had gone through. He was definitely dead and buried; so how could He have come back to life? Mind you they had had high hopes that Jesus was the promised Messiah; but these had been dashed beyond all imagining and reasoning. In the middle of their argument, a man appears, falls into step beside them and, content to go unrecognised, joins in their conversation. They are so wrapped up in their questions and musings that they do not ask his name; but they welcome his contribution and invite him to continue the conversation over supper. Only then in the breaking of bread do they recognise their risen Lord, and find that they, too, have a gospel to proclaim.

One of the strengths of our faith is that we are invited to think and use our God-given minds to discuss and ask questions, whether it be in our study groups or in discussion with our ministers and teachers. Paul's letters are full of arguments justifying the faith, and answering the questions posed by the young churches, e.g. questions about the resurrection and the return of Christ; moral issues, and even food. Theology is based on reasoning. The claims of faith have produced the so-called proofs for the existence of God, and many arguments about the problems of evil and suffering, and the relation between science and religion. It is fascinating to explore these problems in a detached sort of way. They can provide us with an armoury of arguments for any discussion we may get into with non-believers; although none of them are a substitute for the actual experience of meeting the risen Lord, as the Emmaus disciples found.

When the presence of evil and suffering in our lives affects us personally, then we find the road of reason runs alongside the garden of grief, and gives rise to bitter questions. How can an all-powerful, all-loving being allow evil? Why does a young person, full of the promise of life, die tragically? Why do the perpetrators of evil get away with it? Where is God? We can become disappointed and disillusioned. C. S. Lewis in his book *Grief observed* tells of his experience of grief at the death of his wife. It was not just the tears, the fears, the agony, but the anger, the desolation and frustration which culminated in the question 'Where is God?'

Michael Mayne in his book *A year lost and found* gives an excerpt from a novel by Peter de Vries about a father whose severely ill young daughter dies suddenly on her birthday in hospital. He has taken her a birthday cake, but when he learns of her death he goes to the church, and throws the cake with all his strength at the figure of Christ on the cross outside the central doorway. 'It was a miracle enough that the pastry should reach its target after all ... the more so that it should land squarely just beneath the crown of thorns. Then through scalded eyes I seem to see the hands free themselves of the nails and move slowly towards the soiled face. Very slowly, but very deliberately with infinite patience, the icing was wiped from the eyes and flung away.' Michael Mayne writes, 'At Calvary God in Christ invites us to vent our anger and our rage upon Him, in order that we may discover in Him a love that is stronger than our hate.'

Mary's grief in the garden was pure emotion. But the Emmaus disciples demanded answers. So often, in our own lives one runs into the other, and each has a legitimate reaction. It is good to let the tears flow and the questions pour out. Lo, Jesus meets us in the tears and in the questions. He travels with us through our grief and anger, until our hearts burn within us, and we recognise Him as our risen Lord. Then He brings balm to our grief, and His Love shines through our angry questions.

Joan A. Bidwell's poem 'Supper being ended' with its allusions to Emmaus and the Last Supper, encapsulates this experience.

In the quiet place
at close of day
he washes the feet of my mind
from the dust of its fret.

His infinite eyes
see the straining and wounds of the road,
his hands
bring smarting
and cleansing
and balm.

The grace of his health
restores my soul
her place in the circling stars of perpetual praise.

Then, taking again the seamless robe,
the Alpha-Omega,
Master and Lord,
we talk together,
friend and friend.

Lo, Jesus meets us in the world of work.

John 21:1-17

> Seven whole days, not one in seven,
> I will praise Thee.
>
> *George Herbert*

At some point after that first Easter Day, it would appear that the disciples went back to work. Some of them went back to fishing. No doubt; others returned to their usual occupations. I am sure the women returned to their home-making and caring activities. They left the security of the upper room, and returned to Galilee. But what happened? For the fishermen, Jesus barbecued fish after their long night on the Sea of Galilee, and shared breakfast with them. Here they discovered the wonderful truth: that Jesus was with them wherever they were, even when they were immersed in their work. As the women had been told at the empty tomb, if only they had believed it: 'He is not here. He is risen and gone before you.'

In John Masefield's play *The trial of Jesus*, there is a scene in which Procula, Pilate's wife, is waiting anxiously to hear news about the crucifixion of Jesus. Longinus, the centurion, enters and Procula demands that he tell her all that happened. When he has finished she says, 'Do you think that He is dead?' Longinus replies, 'No I don't.' Procula asks, 'Where is He then?' Longinus says, 'Let loose in the world, where neither Jew nor Roman can stop His truth.' David Runcorn puts it another way: 'God is fearfully and gloriously at large in the world.' The glorious truth of Easter means that for those who have met Jesus risen from the tomb, Easter is never over. Every day is resurrection day everywhere.

There is a hymn, by F. Pratt Green, which we often use at the start of worship. Its opening line reads 'God is here, as we His people meet to offer praise and prayer.' It is natural to say

'God is here' when we are gathered to worship Him. But how often do we use these words when we are in the kitchen, the workplace, the supermarket or enjoying our leisure activities? Perhaps we ought to try it sometime!

There is an old country poem by Anna de Bary about a gardener who was aware of the presence of Jesus at all times as he worked.

> He never pushed the garden door,
> He left no footmark on the floor;
> I never heard 'Un stir nor tread
> And yet His hand do bless my head,
> And when 'tis time for work to start
> I takes Him with me in my heart.

Other people accustomed to a more hectic style of life have also spoken of their awareness of Jesus. A famous actress friend frequently mentioned her conversations with the Almighty which she held on a day to day basis. A leading politician, when asked if he was a Christian politician, replied thus: 'When I was a schoolboy, I was a Christian; when I was an apprentice I was a Christian; when I was a metal-worker, I was a Christian; so why not in politics?' For these people, and countless others, Christ is 'gloriously alive' in their lives. The welcoming reality of the risen Lord breaks through the network of all our human transactions.

However the resurrection creates its own new agenda of responsibilities. In that post-Easter event by the Sea of Galilee, after breakfast Jesus took Peter on one side, and asked him three times, 'Do you love me?' When Peter affirmed that he did, Jesus said, 'Feed my sheep, and feed my lambs' – in other words, be a shepherd to my sheep. This was Peter's resurrection agenda and he, indeed, became the shepherd to the early Church.

I wonder what our resurrection agenda might be following on from our Easter experiences? If we claim to love Jesus, are we not also commanded to take on the role of a shepherd? There is a marvellous job-description in the prophecy of Ezekiel. A shepherd is one who looks after a scattered flock. He tends them, and provides good pasture for them, searches for the lost, binds up the injured and strengthens the weak (Ezekiel 34:16).

Ministers are often thought of as shepherds, the church family being their flock. But not everyone is called to be a minister. For those of us who are not, our resurrection agenda is in a different sphere. Most of us have to leave the security of the upper room of fellowship and fellow Christians, and enter into the noise of the contemporary world. Our sheep are probably outside the church, e.g. in the environment of our workplace, where many people are alien to the faith. Again, if we are involved in voluntary projects, we may find ourselves helping people whose values are at odds with Christian ones; and further, in our social activities we will meet people with a variety of interests and attitudes. Carrying out the role of the shepherd in these situations will take the form of whatever particular gift or talent we possess; and we all have to work out how best we can use those gifts to tend, bind up and strengthen those with whom we share our lives.

Lo, Jesus meets us risen from the tomb in so many ways at Easter. He answers our deepest needs, makes us aware of His presence: and gives us our own resurrection agenda: to feed my sheep, to be a shepherd, and share our encounter with Him in whatever way is appropriate in our workaday world.

In the words of a contemporary blessing: 'Lord send us out in the power of your Spirit to live and work to Your praise and glory.'